How Babies Are Made

How Babies Are Made

HERON
BOOKS

Published by
Heron Books, Inc.
20950 SW Rock Creek Road
Sheridan, OR 97378

heronbooks.com

Special thanks to all the teachers and students who
provided feedback instrumental to this edition.

ISBN: 978-0-89-739212-9

Printed in the USA

15 March 2022

At Heron Books, we think learning should be engaging and fun. It should be hands-on and allow students to move at their own pace.

To facilitate this we have created a learning guide that will help any student progress through this book, chapter by chapter, with confidence and interest.

Get learning guides at
heronbooks.com/learningguides.

For teacher resources,
such as a final exam, email
teacherresources@heronbooks.com.

We would love to hear from you!
Email us at *feedback@heronbooks.com.*

IN THIS BOOK

Chapter 1

Boys' and Girls' Bodies

Chapter 1

Boys' and Girls' Bodies

Boys are different than girls. Their bodies are different. You can't really tell the differences with clothes on. But without clothes they look like this:

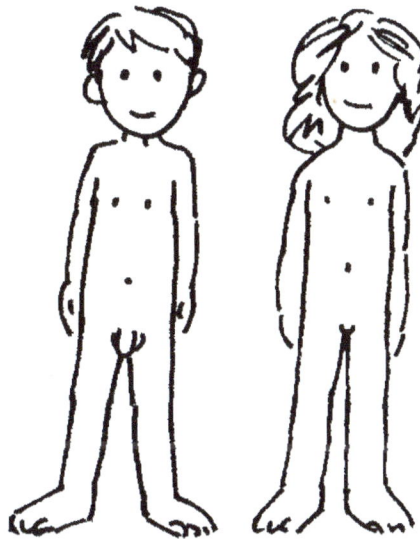

The biggest difference you can see is between their legs. Boys have a body part that hangs there. This part is called a **penis**. Some people call it different names. But its real name is penis. Just behind the penis, boys have something that looks sort of like a little bag with two balls in it. These are called **testicles**.

Girls don't have a penis. They have a small opening between their legs. This is called a **vagina**.

That's one way you can tell boys from girls.

Chapter 2

Men's and Women's Bodies

Chapter 2

Men's and Women's Bodies

Boys and girls grow up and become men and women. Their bodies change as they grow. These pictures show what grown-up people's bodies look like. You can see a woman's body is different from a man's body in several ways.

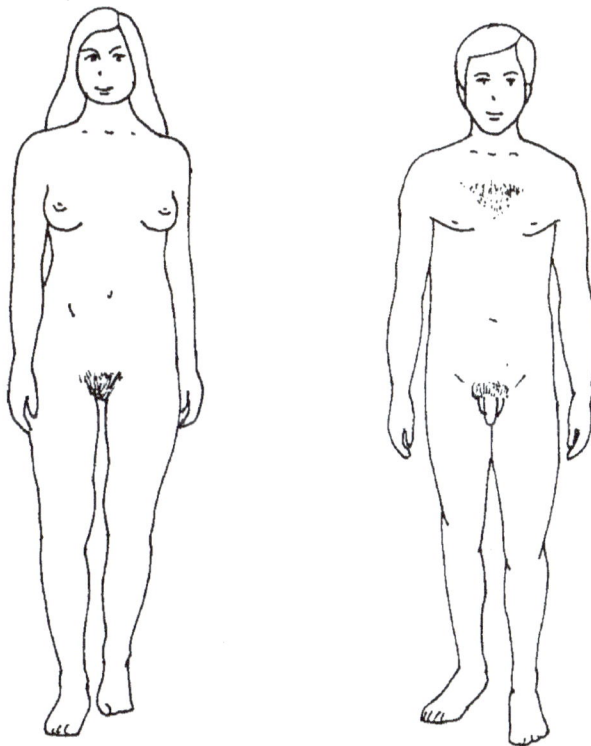

Just like boys, men have a penis and testicles. Boys' bodies grow larger as they get to be men. Their penises and testicles grow, too. A man's penis and testicles are larger than a boy's. You can also see that a man has curly hair in the penis area. Every boy will grow some hair there as he gets to be a man. This usually doesn't happen until he's a teenager.

Look at the woman's body. You can see she also has hair by her vagina. Girls grow hair there as they get to be women. Like boys, girls usually start growing hair sometime when they are teenagers.

Girls have another place that grows as they get to be women. Round bumps, called breasts, grow on their chests.

These are the biggest ways men's bodies are different from women's bodies.

Chapter 3

Who Makes Babies?

Chapter 3

Who Makes Babies?

Have you ever wondered where babies' bodies come from? Some of the other kids may have told you some stories, like a stork or a doctor brings them.

But maybe they told you something not correct because they didn't really understand it themselves. So, here's the truth.

Babies can be made by men and women beginning in their early teen years. Something from one man and one woman are needed to make a baby. A baby can't be made without a man and a woman.

That's why it's important that men and women are different. If there were no men and no women, there would be no baby bodies. Since all people start as babies (you did), it's lucky we have men and women to make the bodies that little people have.

ANIMALS HAVE BABIES, TOO

There are lots of other kinds of babies, too. Animals have babies.

Grown-up animals make babies. Two animals of the same kind make a baby like themselves. Elephant babies are made by grown-up elephants. Cat babies are made by grown-up cats. Some grown-up animals make babies the same way as people.

The two grown-up animals that make a baby have different body parts, just like people. An animal or person with a penis is called a **male**. An animal or person with a vagina is called a **female**. With animals and with people, it takes a male and a female to make a baby.

LET'S DO THIS!
People and Animals with Babies

For this activity you will need:

- paper
- pencil or markers

Steps

1. Draw one picture of people with their baby.

2. Draw four pictures of animals with their babies.

3. Show another person your drawings.

Chapter 4

Making a Baby

Chapter 4

Making a Baby

How do a man and a woman make a baby? Women have eggs inside their bodies. The eggs are in a place in the woman's body called the **ovaries**. You can see them in the picture.

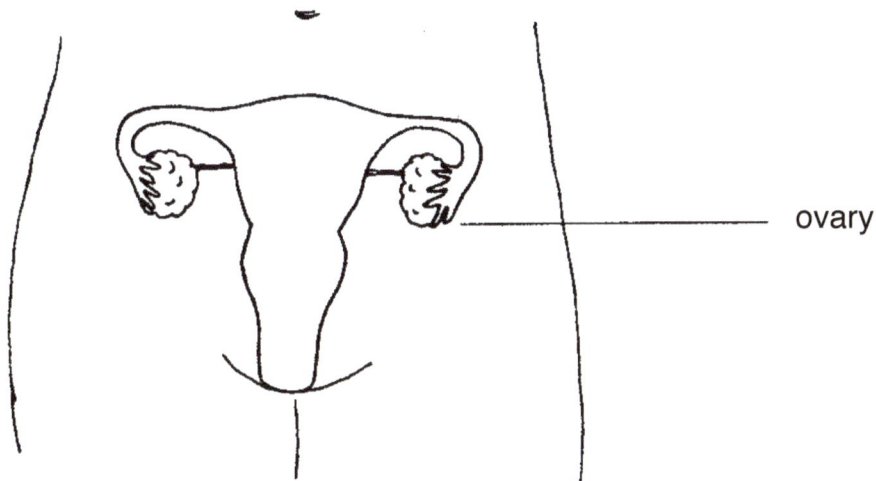

This shows the front.

Eggs are made and stored in the ovaries. Once a month an egg comes out of one of the ovaries and goes through a tube to another place called the **uterus**. It sits there. The vagina connects to the uterus, as shown in the next picture.

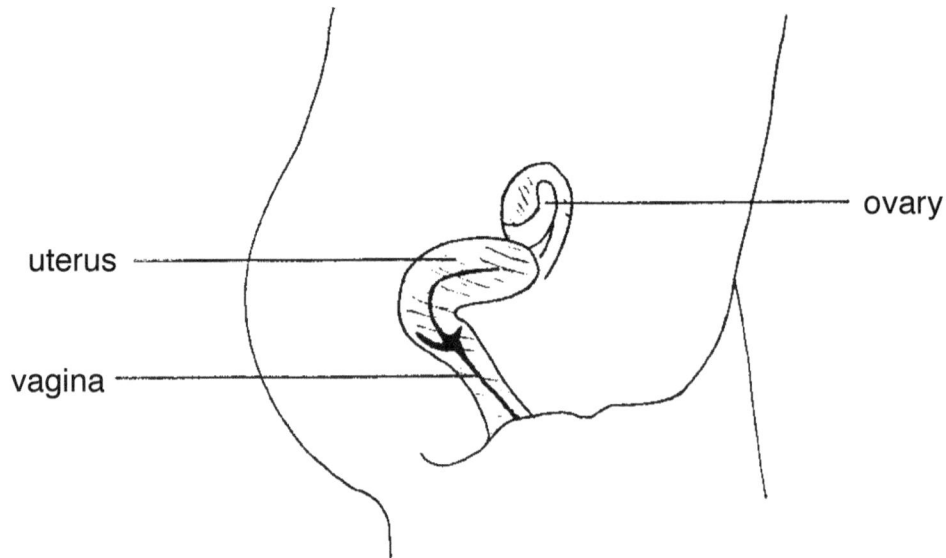

This shows the side.

The egg by itself is not enough to make a baby. It has to come together with something that a man's body makes called **sperm**. A sperm is very, very tiny, and looks something like this:

Notice that the sperm have little tails. The man stores these sperm in his testicles.

Now, to make a baby, the sperm have to get from the man's testicles into the woman's uterus and meet the egg.

To do this, the man and woman have what we call sex. **Sex** means what you do when you make babies.

A man and a woman usually have sex in bed because a bed is comfortable. As the man thinks about having sex, his penis gets bigger than it was and becomes hard and stiff. It sort of stands up. Then, the man puts his penis inside the woman's vagina. It is long and stiff so he can put it in her vagina.

This is the start of having sex. The man moves his penis back and forth inside the woman's vagina. When the man is moving his penis, something happens that starts the making of a baby. Some thick, sticky stuff comes out of the man's penis. His penis is inside the woman, so the stuff goes inside her vagina. This stuff is called **semen**, and in it are lots of the tiny sperm.

Now the sperm have to swim up the vagina almost 8 inches to get to the egg. (Now you know why they have little tails!) Remember, sperm are very tiny and 8 inches is a long way for such a tiny thing to go. Most of them don't make it.

But sometimes a sperm makes it all the way to the egg. The outside of this egg is soft. The sperm goes inside the egg and that's the start of a tiny body!

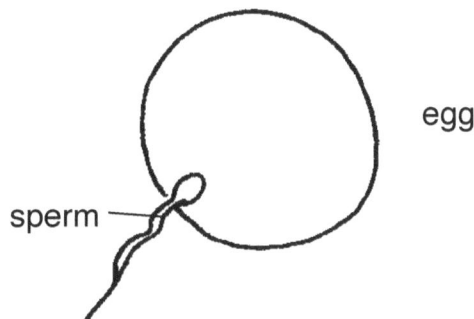

egg

sperm

It grows inside the mother, in her uterus, for about nine months. It grows until it looks like this:

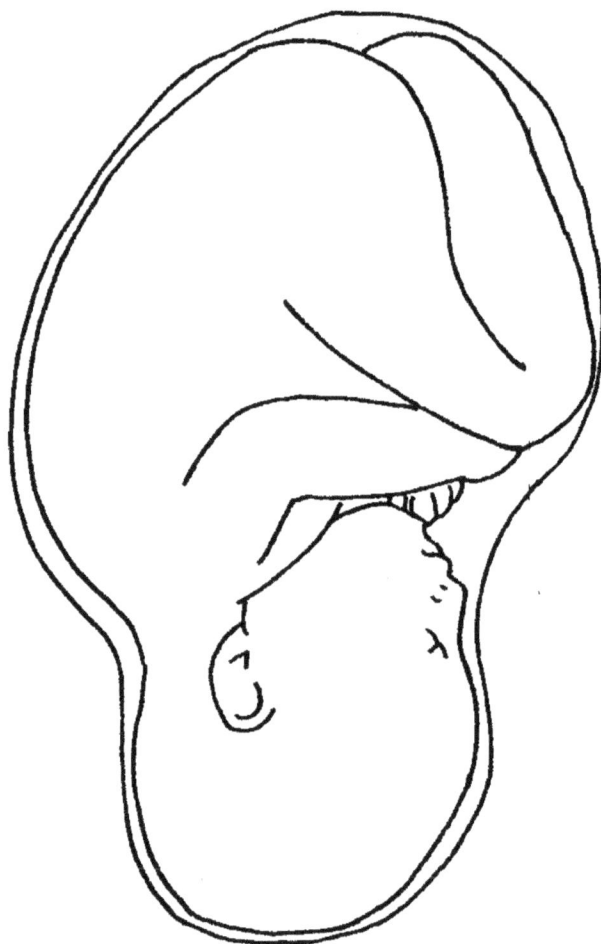

Now the baby is big enough to come out, and the baby is born!

One thing you should know is that every time a man and a woman have sex they don't make a baby. There is an egg in the woman's uterus for only a few days once a month. If there is no egg, no baby can be made. Also, sometimes no sperm make it to the egg. If no sperm gets to the egg, no baby is made. So, it is possible for a man and a woman to have sex without making a baby.

HOW BABY ANIMALS ARE MADE AND GROW

Some animals, like cats, rabbits, dogs, cows, elephants, horses, mice, bats, and whales, have sex much the same as people. The male animal puts his penis in the female animal's vagina. Sperm come from the penis and one gets to the egg to start the baby.

Baby animals grow for different amounts of time inside the mother. A cat baby grows for about two months inside the mother before it's born. A dog baby also grows for about two months. A cow baby grows for about 10 months, a whale baby for about 12 months (one year), and an elephant baby for about two years! As you can see, the bigger the animal, the longer the baby usually grows inside the mother before it's born.

One other thing happens a bit differently, especially in smaller animals. Female animals have more eggs ready at one time for sperm to reach them. If the mother has three eggs and a sperm gets to each, three babies' bodies are started. If the mother has six eggs ready and a sperm gets to each, six babies are started. So, some animals usually have more than one baby. Sometimes people do, too, but not very often.

People usually feel different than animals about having sex. Usually, it's nicer for them if they have sex with someone they love. In fact, people use another name for having sex. Sometimes, they call it "making love."

LET'S DO THIS!
Draw Making a Baby

For this activity you will need:

- butcher paper several feet long
- pencil

Steps

1. Draw vertical lines on the butcher paper that separate it into three fairly equal parts.

2. Label the first part #1 Making a Baby.

3. In this section, draw a picture of sperm swimming up the vagina to the uterus, and show one of them meeting the egg.

4. Show your teacher.

5. Save your drawing for a later activity.

Chapter 5

How a Baby Grows Inside the Mother

Chapter 5

How a Baby Grows Inside the Mother

The egg and sperm joined together are the size of a tiny dot about as wide as a human hair. This grows to a baby in about nine months. That's pretty amazing. Let's look at what happens.

Inside the egg and the sperm are things that are like messages. They don't have words on them, but they are just like messages because they tell the body how to grow. The messages make the body grow as a boy or a girl, tell what color the eyes and hair will be--things like that. Some of the messages come from the mother in the egg. Some of them come from the father in the sperm. So, the baby usually grows up looking a bit like both.

Very, very slowly the baby grows inside the mother. At first, it's just a dot you can hardly see. Then it starts to grow arms, legs, a nose, and eyes. Then, fingers, toes, elbows and knees grow.

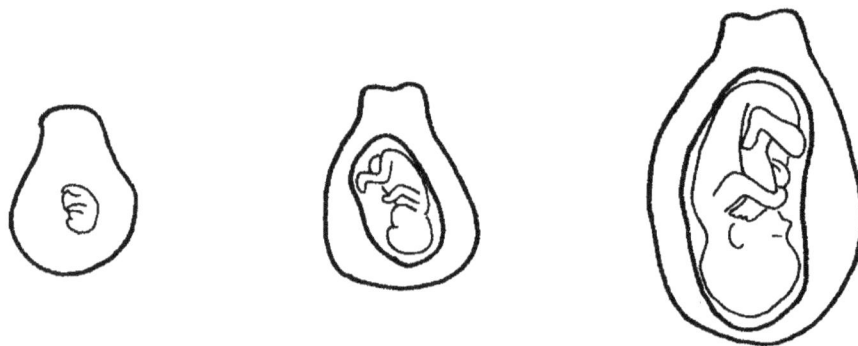

The baby grows inside the mother because it's safe and warm in there. The baby gets its food from the food the mother eats. It doesn't eat it like we do. It gets the food through a tube, called the **umbilical cord**. The tube is attached to the baby's belly at the belly button. The food goes from the mother through the tube to the baby.

The baby keeps growing. It grows hair, toenails, fingernails, eyebrows, eyelashes, and all the things people have.

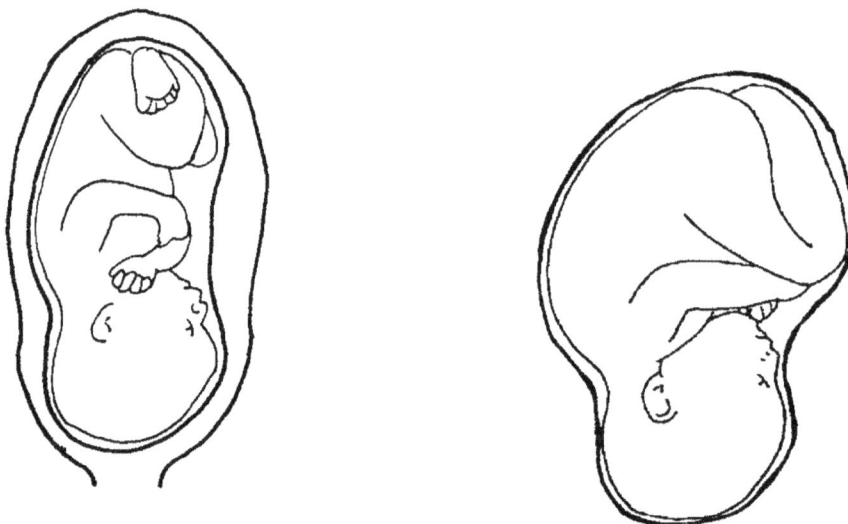

The baby gets big and strong. After about nine months, it's too big to stay inside its mother. By this time, it looks like the mother has a really big stomach.

It's time for the baby to come out!

The baby starts pushing and the mother's muscles start pushing. They push harder and faster. The mother usually goes to the hospital so a doctor can help, but sometimes mothers have their babies at home, or in a special place made just for giving birth.

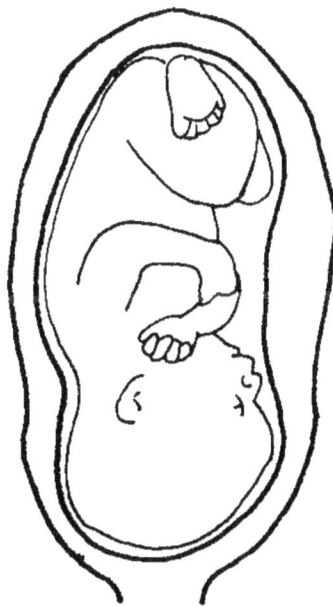

The mother has to push the baby out through the vagina hole between her legs. This hole stretches and gets bigger when the baby is going to come out. The baby usually comes out head first because that's easiest. It's lots of work to push the baby out, but finally it happens.

Then, there is one more thing to do. Remember the umbilical cord that the baby gets food through? Well, now that the baby is born it will get food through its mouth, so it doesn't need the tube anymore.

The doctor cuts off all but a little piece and puts a little clamp on it. This doesn't hurt, and what's left is a little piece of the cord in the middle of the baby's tummy. After a week or so, this little piece dries up and falls off. What's left is the baby's belly button! You got your belly button the same way.

Now, while the baby was growing in the mother's body, her breasts were getting larger. This happens because they were getting ready to make and store milk that the baby can drink. So, if the mother wants to, she can feed her baby after it is born. It gets the milk by sucking on her breast. This is called breast feeding. Many animal babies also get milk from their mother in the same way.

All of this is the way a baby grows inside its mother's body and is born. Your body and your mom's and dad's, even your grandmother's and grandfather's—every person's body—all started growing in this same way!

LET'S DO THIS!
Draw a Baby's Growth and Birth

For this activity you will need:

- your drawing from the Draw Making a Baby activity

Steps

1. On your saved drawing, label the second section #2 Growth of a Baby.

2. In this section, make a drawing showing the growth of a baby.

3. Label the last section #3 Birth of a Baby.

4. In this section, make a drawing showing the birth of a baby.

5. Show your teacher your full drawing and answer any questions.

www.ingramcontent.com/pod-product-compliance
Lightning Source LLC
Chambersburg PA
CBHW041433040426
42450CB00023B/3480